The Tree of Wisdom

By Nagarjuna

Copyright © 2020 Lamp of Trismegistus. All rights reserved. No part of this publication may be reproduced or transmitted in any form or by any means, electronic or mechanical, including photocopying, recording, or by any information storage and retrieval system, without permission in writing from Lamp of Trismegistus. Reviewers may quote brief passages.

ISBN: 978-1-63118-470-3

Studies in Buddhism

Other Books in this Series and Related Titles

Buddhist Psalms by Shinran (978-1-63118-465-9)

The Path of Light: A Manual of Mahayana Buddhism by L. D. Barnett (978-1-63118-471-0)

Psalms of Solomon by King Solomon (978-1-63118-439-0)

The Old Past Master by Carl H. Claudy (978-1-63118-464-2)

Fortune-Telling by Playing Cards by Astra Cielo (978-1-63118-467-3)

The Rosicrucian Chemical Marriage by Christian Rosenkreuz (978-1-63118-458-1)

The Machinery of the Mind by Dion Fortune (978-1-63118-451-2)

Arcane Formulas or Mental Alchemy William Walker Atkinson (978-1-63118-459-8)

Magical Essays and Instructions by Florence Farr (978-1-63118-418-5)

The Human Aura: Astral Colors and Thought Forms William Walker Atkinson (978-1-63118-419-2)

Crystal Vision Through Crystal Gazing by Achad (978-1-63118-455-0)

American Indian Freemasonry by A. C. Parker (978-1-63118-460-4)

The Gospel of the Nativity of Mary by St. Matthew (978-1-63118-448-2)

Ghosts in Solid Form by Gambier Bolton (978-1-63118-469-7)

Thirty-One Hymns to the Star Goddess by Achad (978-1-63118-422-2)

Ancient Mysteries & Secret Societies by M. P. Hall (978-1-63118-410-9)

The Secrets of Enoch by Enoch (978-1-63118-449-9)

Audio Versions are also Available on Audible and iTunes

Table of Contents

Preface...7

*The Commentary of Manners Called
The Tree of Wisdom*...11

PREFACE

The SHE-RAB DONG-BU (Tree of Wisdom) is a metrical translation in Tibetan of a Sanskrit ethical work entitled Prajnya Danda, written by Nagarjuna who flourished in the fourth century of the Buddhist era (about 100 B.C.), The Tibetan version was probably made about the 11th century of our era but the exact date has not been determined. The Tibetan translator describes it as the second volume but I cannot say whether the remainder of the work has been preserved in Tibetan--the Sanskrit original is apparently lost.

When this work was selected as one of the textbooks for the Higher Proficiency Examination in Tibetan, the Tibetan text was edited by the late Rai Bahadur Sarat Chandra Das and printed in continuous lines as is done in Tibet. This adds to the difficulties of the student as there is nothing to show where one verse ends and the next begins. No English translation was prepared at that time, and the present attempt has been made with the object of assisting future students of Tibetan.

The poem is known by name to the educated classes in Tibet but few laymen appear to have read it and fewer still to understand the many obscure passages. In the course of two years spent in Tibet I sought the assistance of monks and laymen in and around Gyantse but only succeeded in finding one elderly scholar who had read the poem. The Abbot of the Palkor Monastery was good enough to make enquiries at Trashi Lhunpo regarding the possible existence of a commentary on this work, but without success. By the courtesy of the Tibetan Trade Agent at Gyantge, Khenchung Lobzang Chungne Lotsawa, the printed text was compared with the xylograph edition forming part of the Ten-gyur collection in the Palkor Monastery and a number of errors detected. It must, however, be added that the Palkor text does not appear to be absolutely accurate. All that can be claimed for the present edition is that it is more correct than the earlier printed text.

Rai Bahadur Sarat Chandra Das remarked in his preface that the She-rab Dong-bu was "largely quoted by Tibetan authors" but it is hardly quotation in the ordinary sense of the word. Later writers have borrowed many of the sentiments and sometimes entire lines, inserting them in their own compositions. This is particularly the case in the Sakya Leg-she (Sans. Subhashita Ratna Niti Nama Shastra), written by the celebrated Kun-gah Gyaltsen in the 13th century of our era, which is said to be a rechauffé of the works of three earlier writers on the same subject. I mention this here as the works of Nagarjuna appear to have been not so much the subject of quotation as the source of extensive literary piracies.

The present translation was made at Gyantse, but the number of passages to which no clear meaning could be assigned by the Tibetans was so great that I was in doubt whether it would be possible to proceed with publication, until I came to Gangtok and obtained the invaluable assistance of Kazi Dawa Samdup, Head Master, Bhutia Boarding School. Kazi Dawa Samdup had the advantage of receiving a scholarly explanation of the first 102 verses from a learned Lama Ge-she

Kachen Tundrup of Shigatse, who studied the book some years ago and was accordingly able to give the meaning assigned by tradition to some of the passages which appear quite incomprehensible at first sight. The latter part of the translation was done without this special advantage and some of the more difficult passages remain to be properly explained. The extreme baldness of the translation is intentional.

I take this opportunity of recording my gratitude to the many Tibetan gentlemen who assisted me at the start, and above all to Kazi Dawa Samdup, without whose assistance this translation would never have seen the light. Finally I would acknowledge my obligation to the Hon'ble Sir Asutosh Mookerjee Sind the Calcutta University who have undertaken the printing of the text and translation.

W. L. CAMPBELL.
GANGTOK, SIKKIM:
October, 1918.

THE COMMENTARY OF MANNERS CALLED THE TREE OF WISDOM

(I do) Obeisance to the Three Deities

* * *

1. Evil persons should be brought under control.
The wise should be reverenced.
Fill your treasury with honest deeds
(And) protect your own countrymen.

2. (As regards) your own secrets and those of others,
If you guard these as your own dear child
He for whom all earthly things are equal
Will make love for man the principal affection.

3. If your wife is evil and your friend evil,
If the King is evil and your relatives evil,
If your neighbor is evil and the country evil,
(Then) abandon them for a distant (land).

4. Avoid that friend who is greedy for wealth.
Avoid a wife who is fond of fornication.
If unskillful in curing and hard to please (or respect)
Avoid such a doctor.

5. Although you know the difference between good and bad deeds
You should carry out your work after consultation.
Although you may only succeed partially
Even without succeeding you are to be admired.

6. The steadfast who speak in few words and politely
Are very much respected by mankind.
As the sun which coming out from the shadow
By his rays creates great heat.

7. (As regards) these doctrines, though you may suffer
(Yet) be not anxious in your mind.
When the moon has been eclipsed
Will it not shine again?

8. Just as for the garlands on the altars
Only full-blown flowers are gathered,
So a gardener, in the same way,
Does not uproot the plant.

9. Rewards and royal favors,
The price of prostitution and praise (from pupil),
The hire of a boat and the rent of a dwelling,
These may be asked for at once
For these six are not to be had after a long interval.

10. A magic spell misunderstood is poison.
Indifference to illness is poison.

An old man keeping company with woman is poison.
A poor man's sleep in the daytime is poison.

11. Worthy men who do not make many promises,
But if a promise is made under pressure
Then it is like a carving on stone.
Even should they die it is not altered.

12. You will come to terms with your enemy on occasion
And on occasion you will quarrel with your friends.
Having learned to distinguish what should be done and what not,
The clever man will always select his opportunity.

13. If you sin in speech you will be damned.
The parrot, the singing bird and the waterhen,
The silent waterduck which man does not catch--
Their entire accomplishment is keeping silence.

14. If you keep your weapons in order your enemy will be subdued.
By wearing poor clothes a woman will be subdued.
By treatment illness will be subdued.
Ignorance will be subdued (overcome) by effort.

15. Keep your resolves to yourself as a secret,
Like the body which lies (hid) in the mud.
If it were not that the sprouts attract attention
Who would find the lotus root?

16. Although it may become perceptible
Still a non-existent substance (reality) will not be mentioned.
How could the peacock in the painting eat the jewels?

17. If anyone plans in his mind to do evil
He always uses pleasant words to the other.
When the hunter sees the game to be killed
He sings a sweet song to please it.

18. Whatever your thought (or opinion) may be
It should be clearly impressed on all men's minds.
They are thus brought under your control,
As by the wish-granting gem.

19. It is easy to live by carrying the loads of others.
It is easy to dress in tree-bark in the forest.
It is easier for men to die
Than to spend their days in quarrelling.

20. The root-principle of mankind is not to quarrel.
What would you do with wealth obtained by quarrelling?
What would you do with wealth and life
Obtained by pride and the suppression of good.

21. He who undertakes work which he cannot carry out,
Who vies with the multitude and disputes with the powerful,

Who lets a woman know his thoughts--
The four gods of death sit at his door.

22. Regard not an evil prince.
Regard not deceitful relatives.
Regard not a lustful woman.
Regard not a great sinner.

23. He who can go anywhere
Why should he be injured through his attachment to his own native land?
The evil man says "it is my own well"
And saying thus, drinks the brackish water.

24. A highly learned man
Has two (forms of) felicity.
Either he will abandon all earthly interests
Or else has much which could be abandoned.

25. He whose glory has left him (and)
Whose efforts have become meaningless,
When a holy man becomes impoverished (in this way)
He is unhappy except in a forest.

26. The career of a holy man is of two kinds.
Like a flower waving its head
Which is either honored by all in the world
Or else disappears alone in the forest.

27. Life, which perishes naturally in a moment,
Has this as its essence.
As your actions and intellect are undeveloped
Remain modest in society.

28. An anthill increases by accumulation.
Similarly eye-medicine is used up by distribution.
The to-be-feared grows less by association.
That is the thing to understand.

29. The anthill and honey,
The waxing moon, up to the full,
The possessions of kings and beggars
Increase by gradual accumulation.

30. Do not be excessively covetous.
Great greed entails punishment.
If you are stultified by excessive covetousness
You are like the fox that was killed by the bow.

31. He who always pursues the man who can do something for him
And pays no heed to the man who has done something
Is like the wicked man whose ear was filled with curds.
Such a one has stolen that which was guarded.
[O, Karna, evil-minded like curdled milk,
You have conquered what you should have protected.]

32. Do not go (in search of) excessive fame.

Judge honestly for yourself.
By the fall of the 'bel' fruit into the water
See, the forest was deserted.

33. Do not say things which hurt the feelings (of others).
Do not speak in a very injurious way.
The good man and the armed
Enemy become known.

34. Even if the son of his enemy speaks sweetly
The wise man is not indifferent.
As a poisonous leaf is extremely potent (irresistible)
It will cause injury at any time.

35. Whosoever does benefit to his enemy
With straightforward intention,
By so doing all enemies will arrive at
The state of folding their hands in devotion.

36. In desiring to injure your enemy
Praise his inherent good qualities.
What do evil thoughts of injury do?
They injure you and not your enemy.

37. Be firm with the unruly, not with mildness
But with suitable harshness.
If the children are not diligent
Does not the beneficent father threaten punishment?

38. As long as you watch the 'way,'
As long as your steps are steady,
As long as your wisdom is unimpaired,
So long is there profit for you.

39. If you are always seeking your own advantage
What is the use of remaining among the multitude?
There exists no means whatever for
Making all beings rejoice exceedingly.

40. To seek from others and yet wish for good food,
To spend your life in begging and yet have great pride,
To be ignorant of literary works and yet wish to dispute,--
These three make you ridiculous to others.

41. The fire which burned the forest
Became the companion of the wind,
And that same extinguished the fire.
So has the weak man no friends.

42. Not doing harm to others,
Not bowing down to low people,
Not abandoning the path of virtue,--
These are small (points) but (really) very many.

43. Having no fear of disease,
Endeavoring to associate with the holy,
Not using the (vulgar) language of the mean,--
A day (spent thus) is greater than a hundred years.

44. Whenever the mean find a little wealth
They despise everybody and are filled with pride.
But the virtuous, although they may attain the possession of wealth,
Remain bowed like ripe rice.

45. Low class creatures,
Should they become possessed of wealth or science,
Think only of quarrelling with everybody
Like the fox with the blue skin.

46. If they become possessed of wealth or learning
Low people become proud.
But even when doubly honored
The wise man will become the more humble.

47. Trade without profit, quarrelling with those who have a following,
Despising to beg (and thus) poor, delighting in lust,
Using rough language to young women,--
These five are improper conduct in a man.

48. The peacock, although scorched by heat in summer,
Would rather hope for rain from the middle of the sky
Than bend its proud neck to the bad water of the dirty pond.

49. The ti-ti-ra bird preserves its own life (somehow) with dew drops,
For it fears to be placed under an obligation by begging
And will not even beg from Indra.

50. If you understand Real Truth, why have a teacher?
When the disease is cured, what is the use of the doctor?
When the water is crossed, what (use) is the boatman?
What use is a sorcerer to a man without passions?

51. As long as an evil man is weak
So long is he naturally good,
(Like) the waters of a river in autumn
Which can be easily crossed by everyone.

52. Where store is made by the mouse,
Where the cat guards the butter,
And the crow is the director of ceremonies--
How could reliance be placed in such an arrangement?

53. If there is much discussion about anything
All make boast of their skill,
And as all wish to be placed foremost
That gathering is brought to naught.

54. Copulation by day and sleeping by day,
Fresh beer, curds and young people drinking,
Sleeping with withered old women,--
These six waste the bodily strength.

55. He whose anger causes no fear,
Who, when pleased, can confer no benefit,
Who can neither destroy nor subjugate--
What avails the anger of such a man?

56. The encounter with the time of misfortune and disease,
A time of famine and danger from enemies,
Being at the king's gate or in Yama's abode,--
These are the common remedy (i.e. affect all alike).

57. (People) strive for worldly things because they want them.
It is not done for the sake of righteousness.
Like the calf which, seeing that the milk is exhausted,
Leaves the cow at a distance.

58. Separation from the object of affection, the contempt of one's own people,
To be much in debt, association with the evil,
To be abandoned by friends who see your poverty,
These five are not fire yet they burn the body.

59. He who, when small discords increase,
Does not attempt to make peace,
Is like the bee's honey leaking in drops,
And the ruin of a country.

60. He who has knowledge is firm.

The holy, even when destitute, do not discard moral virtues,
Although scorched by the sun's natural heat
The natural cold of snow is not taken away.

61. Those who wish to terminate their sins believe in Buddha.
Those who wish to terminate their earthly existences associate with the evil.
Those who wish to terminate their families beget fools and idiots.
When cereals are to be consumed the stomach becomes heated.

62. Those blinded by desire do not perceive their sin.
The blind man does not see the shape of (things).
The proud do not perceive their faults.
He who regards himself (the egotist) does not perceive Real Truth.

63. A conqueror, a water channel, a creeping plant,
Women and the blind, these five,
How they are led by the crafty!
And this leading places them in the power of others.

64. The misery which follows pleasure
Is the pleasure which follows misery.
The happiness and misery of mankind
Revolve like a wheel.

65. The invisible appears before you
And again becomes invisible.
What is that of yours and what are you?
Who will be miserable on that account?

66. Thus the logs of wood
Which go down together to the great ocean
Are driven apart by every wave.
Who will be miserable on that account?

67. The very wise man conquers rather by forcefulness than by anger.
The evil man fails by being angry.
Oh, evil men, defeated by defeat,
How could you be called to the society of the wise?

68. A big stone, by a great effort,
May be thrown to the top of a hill,
But can be toppled over by a small (effort).
Our own faults and virtues are like this.

69. The man who, with regard to something which is not to be done,
Meddles in the matter
Will surely come to grief,
Like the monkey which turned out the child.

70. He who has entirely forsaken his own interests

And rejoices in those of the other party
Will surely be destroyed.
How such a man resembles King Rab-mar!

71. If an astronomer calculates from the sky
He will ascertain the paths of the moon and the stars;
But in his house the womenfolk are at variance,
And he does not perceive their various misconduct.

72. The moon's color was apparent (reflected) in the unsullied water,
And you wished to seize the lotus root.
Oh, swan, who knew how to separate water and milk,
What has become of your knowledge to-day?

73. Any man who has work, great or small,
And desires to do it,
And in this endeavor does his best,
Is considered to be doing a lion's work.

74. So, in protecting his kingdom
And in overcoming his venturesome rivals,
(A king) should not rely on his subjects
But do it personally in this present life.

75. He who says to himself, 'who is the loved one and who the other,'
Who acts affectionately, magnanimously
And broadmindedly, such a man

Controls the whole earthly globe.

76. By always uttering pleasant speeches
It is easy for a king to beguile his people.
But as regards profitable words, which are like medicine,
The speaker is rarer than the listener.

77. If you understand the purport of the doctrine
As when the beam is at fault when weighing is done,
Even if it was constructed by a reputed wise man,
It is better to let your own (conviction) be the winner.

78. If he is equal in wealth and ability,
If he knows the essential vital point and is diligent,
A follower of this kind is sure to injure you.
No enemy will injure you as he will.

79. If fire is lighted in water
How is it to be extinguished?
If the fear comes from the protector
Who is there to protect you from this fear?

80. (A drum) when not adjusted, does not give forth pleasant sounds.
Even when adjusted the sound emitted is not sweet.
The world is like a small drum.
It should be so adjusted as to give forth a melodious sound.

81. The lord of the earth, being influenced by passionate desires, does not discriminate between benefit and injury.

He conducts himself as he pleases, like a lust-maddened elephant.

Tortured by remorse, he falls over the precipice of despondent misery.

He blames those around and is ignorant of his own fault.

82. In a time of disputes a king, rather than acquire wealth,
Should preserve his life by abandoning property.
Just as when the butcher shears the sheep's fleece
(The sheep thinks) the sparing of its life to be a great gain.

83. When there is a snake at the root and an eagle above,
Monkeys climbing in the branches and the flowers surrounded by bees,
Where a resting place is provided for all savage animals,
Pay no heed to (beware of) such a sandalwood tree.

84. By whatever means you control your enemies
It is not the (physical) ability but the method (which matters).
See how the crow with the string of golden beads
Got the snake killed.

85. He who has understanding is mighty.
What can you do with might without understanding?
How strong the lion was,
Yet he was killed by the hare.

86. If you (want to) have proper method in your work
Consult those possessed of understanding.
What need is there to speak of obtaining health, wealth and happiness?
Even if you fail it will still look well.

87. The conduct of the morally virtuous is self-evident,
But how can it cure evil persons?
Like phlegm (? acidity) which is brought on by hot rough-tasting condiments (their evilness) becomes very much increased.

88. The man against whom you feel anger in your heart
Is not to be admonished by words.
Catch your enemy by the feet and
Then admonish him with the weapon of words.

89. In as far as danger has not been encountered
In so far is danger to be feared.
At the time of real danger
It should be vanquished like a mistake (which is acknowledged).

90. (As regards) one who has imbibed the truth,
Is it clever to impose upon such a man?
When a man is resting on the bamboo
[When a man is resting in the embraces of a beautiful woman]

What is brave about killing him?

91. Even when young, rejoice in the intense tranquility of the old.
Be not proud of what you know, even when learned.
However great your glory, be forbearing in your manner.
However high you may rise, be not proud.

92. Those who ever delight to benefit all creatures
Are supreme like the lamp made from a jewel,
Which relies not on oil
Nor on the vessel nor on the wick (for its light).

93. A doctor taking food and not digesting it,
A king speaking falsehoods, and
A man of good birth misbehaving himself,
These three are very unbecoming.

94. By association with the exalted,
Who would not become exalted?
The thread on which the flowers are strung as a garland is attached to the head.

95. He who preaches at the timely season
And speaks when opportunity arises
Will be very much remarked
And obtain worldly greatness.

96. He who is possessed of diligence, courage,

Might, wisdom, (the power) to subdue others,
And perseverance, these six virtues,
Is feared even by the gods.

97. (As regards) your former enemy, now defeated,
Trust him not even when he wishes to become your friend.
See how in the cave where the owls were gathered
The raven lit a fire and they were burned.

98. Eating, sleeping, fearing and copulating--
Man and the brutes are alike in these.
By the practice of religion mankind is elevated
If religion is not understood, is man not on a level with the brutes?

99. Those who speak ill of religion,
Although they go and come by day,
Are like the smith's bellows:
They have breath but they are not alive.

100. Leaving the patron, Buddha,
And bowing to other gods,
Is like a fool who comes to the bank of the Ganges
And being thirsty digs a well.

101. Although you may remain in a country for a very long time
It is absolutely certain that you will have to leave
Whatever may be the difference in the parting.

The actual going cannot be avoided.

102. By compulsory separation excessive pain is infinitely caused to the mind.
But if the giving-up is voluntary
Infinite peaceful happiness will be obtained.

103. One's desire is to be attractive and happy,
And wealth is of course pleasant.
But yet this world of existence
Is like a healthy drunken person being carried.

104. For living beings there is no moral defilement equal to lust.
Nothing injures others as envy does,
None is so fawning as a beggar,
There is no friend or relative to equal generosity.

105. There is no eye like (that of) wisdom,
There is no darkness like spiritual darkness,
There is no enemy like disease,
There is no danger to equal death.

106. Comparing these, the most inexorable
Is death, which will certainly come.
(Therefore) let your mind be turned from desire
And rejoice in the True Religion.

107. It is well to have this friend and that gem.

The wishing gem is real--stones are not gems.
The topaz being treated as the best (of gems),
Such a gem (causes) the ruin of the world.

108. Whatever there be on the earth's surface, grain,
Gold, cattle and good health,
Not all these will suffice to satisfy one man.
If you understand this you will obtain tranquility.

109. Wealth, hoarded with great pains
And fondled (handled) at intervals,
How it resembles the starving mouse (who hoards his store).
Wealth is merely a source of misery.

110. Earthly life is not stable,
Wealth and enjoyment are not stable,
Wife and child are not abiding,
(Therefore) trust in religion and (good) reputation.

111. A king is not satisfied with great riches,
A clever man is insatiable for elegant sayings,
The ocean is never sated with water,
The world has never enough of the sight of beauty,
Fire is not to be satisfied with wood,
Nor (is it possible) to satisfy a child's desires.

112. Moral conduct, self-restraint,
And the control of the mind,--

Whoever bears these earnestly in mind
And remains so, then what more does he need?

113. If you remain utterly contented
You are far from the plane of the evil man.
Pleasures which are bound by the ties of carnal desire
Beget trouble at every step.

114. This so-called body, full of faults,
Has however one great moral quality.
Whatever it encounters in this temporal life
Its movements (depend upon) the steersman (you).

115. The forest elephant is powerful although he lives on grass.
The serpent, although he lives on air, is not lean.
The ascetics who have only a little grass and fruit are not of the past (do not die).
Thus, modesty and contentment are the only objects of attainment.

116. Where is the solitary retreat where there is not
Vegetation and dustless water?
The moon is the public light.
What is the use of (personal) property?

117. The surest possession is real contentment.
It is not difficult to earn your livelihood, whatever it may be.

(It is like) places where there are grass, leaves and water.
There is no place where these are not (to be found).

118. The tiger is chief of the forest and the elephant is leader.
Make of the grass your seat and your garments of tree-bark,
And have the fruit of the trees for food.
The evil society of poor relations is not (real) life.

119. The man who, either in a good or bad (style),
Adapts himself somehow to what he has
And continues to keep his body (from impurity),
What is the attraction of wealth to him?

120. With the price of great good actions
The ship of your (present) body has been bought.
So long as it is not wrecked,
Strive to cross the ocean of human misery.

121. For so long as the moon of pleasant times is waxing,
And so long as Death, the planet Saturn, does not find you,
So long live chastely
And let your actions be right actions.

122. When your eyes are fixed in unconsciousness
And you have come to your last breath through constant hiccoughing,
As one led in the dark to a great precipice,
Of what assistance can child and wife be then?

123. He who yearns in pity, whose passions are controlled, who rejoices in contentment,

Who is passionless, rejoices at the general happiness, lives in the woods, eats fallen fruits,

Wears bark on his emaciated body, cries 'victor, victor' in the sweetest fashion (to him who)

At Benares triumphed over the power of death, will yet have to discard this mortal body.

Salvation is not (to be found) in believing in religious books not yet in freedom from bodily suffering.

124. If the thoughts are controlled by wisdom
Then salvation is very near.
To get rid of the contamination of moral faults
What is the use of shaving your head?

125. To him who has no covering for his mind
What is the use of a cotton robe?
He whose mind is imbued with compassion for all sentient beings,
That is (the way of) salvation and divine wisdom.
Ashes and long hair do not constitute the religious robe.

126. He who is subdued in the prime of life
I know for a really subdued person.
If all the senses were completely exhausted (i.e. by age)
How could he possibly not be subdued?

127. Over friends and kindred in the burning place
There comes a change when the smoke has dispersed.
As regards that which (always) accompanies you,
If you are convinced that it is your own works, then practice acts of virtue.

128. Wealth, acquired through great misery
Or by acts contrary to religion,
Or by bending before your enemy,
Such wealth is not proper wealth.

129. The holy man who is very firm in his longing to act nobly
Is always miserable through the fear of being decried in society.
But the shameless man who spreads the root of perverse conduct,
And does not discriminate between the proper and improper is happier on the whole.

130. He who has not the sense to distinguish between the proper and improper,
Who has abandoned all heed and (observance of) vows,
Who only wishes to be filled with good food,
What difference is there between a rich man of this kind and the beasts?

131. The great source of virtues, both visible and invisible, is knowledge.

Therefore, if you are striving to procure them.
Take hold of wisdom in its entirety.

132. A hero is born among a hundred,
A clever man is found among a thousand,
But the wise hero in a hundred thousand
May be born in a thousand (or not at all).

133. By the wise all sciences will be studied even when they are past middle age.
Although there may be no results in this life
It will become easier for them to obtain such in another life.

134. Even when white-haired and wrinkled
Learning from others should be treasured.
Wherever the man of much learning may go
He will not obtain the aggregate (of learning).

135. A king and an accomplished man--
These two are not alike.
A king is esteemed in his own country,
An accomplished man is esteemed everywhere.

136. Although the accomplished man have faults
Philosophers will not grieve.
Although the moon may become spotted (stained)
The firm look at it with pleasure.

137. There is no bodily ornament like accomplishments,
There is no (physical) misery like mental worry,
There is no protection for the body like patience,
There is no relative (or friend) to equal charity.

138. Although the holy man may live far away
His virtues act as a messenger.
Through sniffing the perfume of the kitaka (flower)
The bees are attracted themselves.

139. If you are persevering in virtue
What is the use of your haughty attitude?
The cow which has no milk,
Even if a bell be attached to it, will not be purchased.

140. Our existence is short but science is of many kinds.
We may estimate life but we do not know how (long) it will be.
So, like the swan which separates milk from water,
Devote yourself to whatever you undertake.

141. Although many large stars are gleaming
And the moon too shines as an ornament of the earth, yet
Whenever the sun sets it becomes night.
Except for the sun there is no meaning attached (to the terms) 'east' and 'west'.

142. On whatever it shines
Darkness is dispelled and light produced.

The shining of the sun being supreme
What is there in the shining of the other (bodies)?

143. The man who accomplishes one single act thoroughly
Excels all sentient beings--what need for many (acts)?
As the moon, when full, lights the earth's surface--
A great multitude of stars have not this power.

144. The growth of moral virtue depends on one's self.
(The acquisition of) property depends on previous merit.
Why blame anybody for this?

145. Moral virtues are to be obtained by making an effort,
And as this effort rests with yourself,
To say that others possess moral virtues--
Who could endure to lead such a life?

146. Of those who understand the meaning of the scriptures
There are many even among the crippled.
It is a matter for rejoicing to find the sharp-pointed sword by which the enemy is conquered.

147. Rich men are to be found even among the barbarians
And there are many heroes among the beasts,
But holy men who can explain the various truths are the rarest of all.

148. There are not sandalwood (trees) on all hills,

Nor does one get pearls from all elephants.
The learned who can explain the meaning of the Real
Are not to be found everywhere.

149. Real Truth is a virtue to the talented
But a harmful thing to those without talent.
The water of the river is very free from impurity;
But, entering the ocean, it becomes undrinkable.

150. The cultured delight in culture:
The uncultured find no pleasure in it.
The bee is attracted from the forest by the lotus.
The frogs, although living together, are not thus.

151. The fame of the sagacious
Increases among the sagacious themselves,
As valuables among experts
And heroes in battle.

152. The swan does not look well in an assemblage of hawks,
Nor the horse among the donkeys,
Nor the lion among the foxes,
Nor the clever man among fools.

153. That which is placed on their heads (i.e. respected) by the great
May be considered (merely as) a basis by the vulgar.
As the 'chorten' to which the learned bow

Is used as a seat by the crows.

154. Though possessing it themselves unproclaimed
While others have it in small measure,
Holy men delight in such moral virtue.
How remarkable is such conduct!

155. The virtues of the omniscient
Are comprehended only by the omniscient.
The exact weight of the earth
Is known only to Ta-ye.

156. If people mutually advertise each others' virtues,
Even he who possesses none will acquire them.
But he who proclaims his own virtues,
Even were he Indra, would not be respected.

157. There where the possession of learning is not respected
  Why should the learned man go (thither)?
  In the city of the naked Jainas
  What would the washerman do?

158. Alas, this stupid world
  Has not obtained personal independence (i.e. initiative),
  But following (imitating) the doings of others
  Is lost in the vessel of the unobstructed.
  [Disappears (like a lump of copper) in a vessel of (molten) copper.]

159. Of the two, the buffoon and the clever man,
To the fool the laughter-maker is superior.
The buffoon acquires wealth
But the learned man goes empty-handed.

160. By means of various records of profitable meaning
The sage passes his time.
The indigence (consequent on) abandoning religion
May be acquired even in sleeping.

161. He who in an assembly of many persons
Makes no effort to obtain the virtues of the holy,
What is the profit in such a one being born who is driven away by his own mother's pains?

162. The way of the wise man is knowledge,
The way of the cuckoo is a sweet note,
The way of the ascetic is patience,
The way of a woman is perversity.

163. Astronomy itself and doctrinal principles,
The Eagle-spell and the repeating of spells,
(Of these) the essential meaning should be seized.
Do not analyze the sound (of the words).

164. Knowledge contained in books
And wealth procured from others,
When the time for needing them arrives,

Are neither knowledge nor wealth.

165. The accomplishments of the teacher of the arts
Are but accomplishments for earning a living,
But the study of the termination of earthly incarnation
Why should that not be the accomplishment?

166. To no man without (due) scrutiny
Should sound advice be given.
See, how for only giving a place to a monkey
The man was made homeless.

167. Some devote themselves to speech (preaching),
Some gain their object without speaking.
The reed-flower has no fruit,
The walnut has both flower and fruit.

168. The fruit of the kataka tree
Clears all water,
But, if its name only be mentioned,
This does not cause the mud in the water to subside.

169. Although a man may be learned in written works,
Yet if he does not apply (what he knows)
(He resembles) the blind man who even with a lamp in his hand cannot see the road.

170. Like the moon which waxes and wanes,
In having recourse to the holy or impious

A little virtue may be increased
Or vast accomplishments may be decreased.

171. It is easier to have a clever man for one's enemy
Than to be friends with the stupid (unlearned).
(As in the stories of) the protection of the Brahmin by a thief
And of the monkey who squeezed the king's eyes.

172. The clever, the disciplined,
The contented and the truth-tellers,
It is better for such to die
Than (to live in) the kingdom of the evil.

173. (In the matter of) a snake's venom and that of an evil man,
An evil man is more venomous than a snake,
For the snake's venom may be overcome by drugs and spells
But what can soothe the venom of an evil man?

174. Although the evil may be benefited by a hundred talents
Yet, even when happy, they use abusive language.
He who is well educated is firm.
Although poor as a faqir he will not abandon virtue.

175. The naturally evil man
Is like the weighing scales--

A little thing sends him up
And a little thing sends him down.

176. Although smeared with sandalwood, musk and camphor
The natural strong smell of garlic is not driven out.
Although many texts may be well studied
One does not drive out the natural evil in one's disposition.

177. There are no lotuses on the face of a holy man's son,
Nor do horns grow on the heads of prostitutes' sons.
But in so far as there was perversion in the act
In so far is that the essential characteristic of the bastard.

178. The word which is uttered is one thing
And different from the thought in the mind.
Alas, then, for the crooked-minded!
Who can change this natural disposition?

179. He assiduously retains his vices
And ever discards the moral virtues.
In retaining vice and discarding virtue
The evil man resembles a strainer.

180. He who has been refuted by an evil man
Loses confidence even in the holy.
When a child's mouth has been scalded by (hot) milk
He will drink curds only after blowing on them.

181. Seeing the stars' reflection on the lake by night,

The swan is disappointed in taking them for lotus shoots,

So that even when he sees the real lotus shoot by day he will not eat it.

When once refuted by a liar one will doubt even the truthful.

182. A woman's appetite is twice (that of a man),

Her deceitfulness four times (as much),

Her shame six times,

And her passions eight times--so it is said.

183. Not by gifts nor by attentions,

Not by worship nor by veneration,

Not by (constant) association nor by assiduity,--

By none of these is a woman to be resisted (? controlled).

184. When he was carried off by the King of the Birds

The White Lotus Serpent God said:

"He who tells secrets to women

"His life is lost there and then."

185. (By them) one's object and religion are completely destroyed,

They create an obstacle in the attainment of salvation,

They become the cause of all mischief.

Rather therefore avoid other men's womenfolk.

186. If even one written verse (of truth)

Is given by a Lama to his pupil,
The gift given would be supreme.
Such a thing is not on earth.

187. All worldly pleasures should be abandoned,
But, if you are unable to abandon them,
Then cling to the holy.
That is the cure for it.

188. All desires should be abandoned,
But, if you cannot abandon them,
Let your desire be for salvation.
That is the cure for it.

189. The unhelpful relative is like a stranger,
But he who helps, even if he be an outsider, is a relative.
Like the body and its diseases which are with us
And the beneficial medicine of solitude.

190. If you hold, with assiduity,
A pot half full of water
On your head; so also if respected
The evil man becomes excited (angry).

191. Whatever may be agreeable to your mind,
Although it be far away is yet near.
That which is not kept firmly in mind,
Although by your side is yet afar off.

192. Though we may live in the society of the impious
There is no intimacy like the water and the lotus.
The holy may ever live far apart,
Yet they rejoice like the moon and the water-lily.

193. If you are ever desirous of friendship
Then do not do these three:
Laying wagers, money transactions,
And speaking privily with women.

194. When milk is got from a horn,
When the reed-flower drops honey,
Then, when a woman is true,
The lotus will grow in dry ground.

195. A man possessed of very little moral merit,
Even should he obtain abundance, knows not how to enjoy it,
Like a dog on a lake of snow (glacier)
Which, when thirsty, licks with its tongue.

196. Those who do work in this world
Would not properly carry provisions for the journey without payment;
But beggars and the poor, without its being evident.
Have a hundredfold profit in the future.

197. As we have to go, leaving wealth behind,
Therefore men give alms.

As, even if you die your property is not lost,
Realize that giving alms is like (the act) of a (clever) miser (? economist).

198. Hesitating to impoverish themselves by charity,
The miserly do not give alms.
But this (wealth) being the real danger
The learned man distributes his wealth.

199. From your food, why not give about half to the beggars?
The desire and the reward which charity brings
Will be obtained at some time.

200. Although you may get no results from your actions, still do not be grieved,
For you can still give alms from what you possess.
Leaves, flowers, fruit, water and medicines,
All these can ultimately be rendered inimitable by the power of mental dedication.

201. (As regards wealth) which is devoid of charity and enjoyment (neither given away nor enjoyed),
To be the owner of such wealth is to err.
For although it is your own property
Why are you not the owner (why don't you use it ?)?

202. Further, this is the place (lit. earth) for action,
The beyond is the place for results.

Whatever may be done here,
That same will certainly be enjoyed there (i.e. the fruit).

203. The wealth, rank, beauty and health of others,
Why be grieved in seeing these here (below)?
If you desire these, is not the getting of the fruits
of work from the seed of virtuous action applicable to you too?

204. If you have possessions and do not distribute them,
What is the use of keeping them by you?
The fruit of the kimpaka
May grow, but what is its use in hunger?

205. Whoever gives alms which do not harm others--
His various (resulting) pleasures will neither be carried away by water
Nor burned by fire nor stolen by thieves.
Such possessions will never be utterly destroyed.

206. He who does not try a remedy for the disease of Hell (i.e. of the going to Hell),
When he reaches the place where there is no medicine
What will he do--he and his disease?

207. Holy men are seized by the snake of words which comes from the pit of savage men.
As a means of allaying this poison
Drink the medicine of wisdom and patience.

208. Although you may kill all your life long
You will not exhaust (the number of) your enemies.
But if your own anger be slain,
That is to slay the real enemy.

209. The mighty are not amenable to reform,
Therefore why exercise patience (with them).
With, those who are disciplined and peaceful in conduct
What necessity is there for patience?

210. If you are merely angry owing to an injury,
Then why not be angry with anger which obviously destroys religious aims and salvation?

211. He who, having seen the excellence of others,
Is afflicted by disturbance in his own mind,
Will not gain even a little of the Truth.
Such a being destroys his own merit.

212. Let all hear this moral maxim,
And having heard it keep it well:
Whatever is not pleasing to yourself
Do not that unto others.

213. As regards the leaving of this mortal life,
Who is not clever in knowing and speaking about it?
But when it comes to practicing (what they preach)

(Those who know) would be considered wise among the sages.

214. Property is unstable, and youth perishes in a moment.
Life is like being ever in the grinning fangs of Death.
Yet (mankind) delays to obtain release from this world.
Alas, the conduct of mankind is very surprising!

215. He who has a good intellect but is lazy,
Such a being will not become exalted.
He is like a youthful writer
Who makes his calculations in the dust.

216. If all these human beings
Could perceive the God of Death on their (own) heads,
Even in food there would be no flavor.
What need to mention other things?

217. The God of Death does not wait to ask whether
your (composite) works are completed or not.
Therefore do to-morrow's work to-day,
And the evening's work in the morning.

218. So long as you are healthy and produce a harvest
Which is not ruined by the great hail of disease,
And so long as your intellect is in your work,
All this is the time for heeding religious doctrines.

219. What are wreaths of flowers to donkeys and cattle?

What is delicate food to quadrupeds and pigs?
Light to the blind or songs to the deaf?
Of what use is religious doctrine to fools?

220. So long as one is not ambitious
For so long will one's accomplishments be great.
If great ambition be entertained in the mind
How can moral attainments be controlled?

221. So long as a man does not beg, even when the time comes,
For so long is he (styled) a glorious ascetic.
Brave, clever, of high rank and
Manly are the terms used (of a man until he begs).

222. The first inventor of anything,
How very wonderful (admirable) he is!
The water-mill having been made,
Can be managed even by a girl.

223. A sage's son may suitably die soon,
And a king's son suitably live for a long time.
For the hunter's son life and death are equally unsuitable, and for the saint's son equally convenient.

224. Then let that which exists in the beginning
For the purpose of increasing man's understanding,
Let the elegant classics be expounded by the man who understands the doctrines.

225. Words of the nature of elegant sayings
Should be collected as far as convenient.
For the temporary but supreme gift of words
Any price will be paid.

226. The student of science, the hero,
And every beautifully formed woman,
Wherever they go
Acquire great fame, there and then.

227. A scientist and a king
Are not to be compared in any way.
The king is esteemed in his own country.
The wise man is esteemed wherever he goes.

228. He who is handsome, youthful, accomplished,
And born of high caste, yet,
Like the flower of the violet-lac tree,
Does not look well when separated from his caste.

229. He who has a body but is devoid of learning,
Even though of good birth, what use is he?
In the world reverence (comes) from learning.
From lack of learning comes destruction.

230. If you desire ease, forsake learning.
If you desire learning, forsake ease.
How can the man at his ease acquire knowledge,

And how can the earnest student enjoy ease?

231. He who is no friend of knowledge
Will always be in misery
He who is a friend of knowledge
Will always obtain happiness.

232. What country is foreign to a sage?
Who is hostile to a pleasant speaker?
What load is heavy to a man in his own home?
What distance is long to the energetic?

233. Since he who gives has friends,
The summit of the king of mountains is not too high,
The earth's profundities are not too deep,
And even when sundered by the ocean it is not beyond (his reach).

234. The superior man who has learned from books (only),
And has not studied (things) from many standpoints,
Resembles a pregnant girl of loose morals.
He does not look well in an assemblage.

235. He who scorns the spiritual teacher (lit. Lama), who has given him even a single letter,
Will pass through a hundred dog-incarnations
And be reborn of low caste.

236. To whomsoever a single letter

Is given by a Lama as to a pupil,
Whatever he may hand over (in payment), there does, not exist sufficient wealth on the earth's surface to repay this.

237. He who brings one up, he who imparts elegant (learning),
He who imparts science,
He who feeds one and gives fearlessness,
These five are declared to be like fathers.

238. The wife of a king or of a minister,
Likewise the wife of a friend,
A brother's wife, and one's own mother,
These five are declared to be like mothers.

239. Counsel (given to) fools
Excites but does not pacify them.
He who pours out milk for a snake
Is only increasing its venom.

240. The fool, who is really a two-footed brute,
Should be specially avoided,
For, like the unseen thorn,
The pain of his words hurts.

241. If a fool sees a fool
He is more refreshed by this than by sandalwood.
If he sees a learned man
He regards him as a patricide.

242. (As regards) benefiting the evil,
Whatever you may do they are not grateful;
But if you do even a small service to a holy man,
For this he is yours to command for life.

243. All the doings of fools are like ripples on water quickly effaced.
(The doings of) a holy man are like a carving on stone.
They may be small but they are permanent.

244. Though the evil man may speak sweetly,
Yet he is not to be trusted.
The peacock has a sweet note,
But for food it eats powerful poison.

245. Alas, the evil man and
Phlegm (mucous) are really alike.
By mildness they are excited
And by roughness (astringent) they are soothed.

246. An evil man, gold, a drum,
A wild horse, women and cloth
Are controlled by beating.
These are not vessels for elegant doings.

247. Association with the evil man is unbecoming,.
Whether he be pleasant or obnoxious.
As with a dog--it is unbecoming whether you play

With him or let him lick you.

248. Wildness is worse than a serpent.
A serpent's venom can be assuaged by drugs and spells,
Wildness is not to be assuaged by anything.

249. The sins of the unruly (undisciplined)
Leave their mark on the temperament.
Whosoever mixes with the unruly
Becomes even more unruly than they.

250. Even without noticing his father's conduct
The son imitates him.
From the kitaka tree
One does not get the kurura fruit.

251. If my father, mother, own brother
And wife imitate me
In whatever sin I commit,
It is as if they had committed it.

252. This earth, the mighty ocean
And the mountains are not a burden,
But he who is ungrateful
Is indeed a heavy burden.

253. He who stays in the society of those of good moral behavior
Rejoices to benefit all evil spirits (elementals).

Although Yama is the destroyer,
Yet wise men praise him very much.

254. In the society of the clever, the disciplined,
The contented, and the truthful,
Imprisonment is a superior state.
The sovereignty of the unruly is not thus.

255. Intimacy in the society of the holy,
Conversation in the society of the learned,
And the friendship of the unselfish,
These will cause no regrets.

256. Although for a very long time
You may not perceive the misery (caused by sin) in this world and the other world,
Yet bring your mind into harmony with religion.

257. Although a thing may afford you mental enjoyment,
Yet, if the full fruition is to be injurious, how can it be right?
If anything upsets your health
How could it be right to eat such a sweet dish?

258. That which hurts but is profitable
Is drunk by the wise like medicine.
The result, attained afterwards,
Becomes in itself incomparable.

259. If a learned king summarizes the meaning (of this book)
In the beginning, the middle and the end,
It will be found to be not otherwise (than stated).

260. When the ocean shall be no more
It may be crossed in the middle, so they say.
Whether holy men exist or not
We should not transgress the moral codes.

www.ingramcontent.com/pod-product-compliance
Lightning Source LLC
LaVergne TN
LVHW041459070426
835507LV00009B/699